UNBREAKABLE

SHARON T. ANDERSON

Fulton Books, Inc.
Meadville, PA

Published by Fulton Books 2020

ISBN 978-1-64654-280-2 (paperback)
ISBN 978-1-64654-281-9 (digital)

Printed in the United States of America

Contents

I'm Coming Out!

Listen! I'm capable of standing on my own two feet, choosing my own path, and giving my own speech. I don't need you to think for me, speak for me, or tell me what to believe. So take a step back, and let me breathe. Before our encounter, I used to cherish the color blue. Now that shade reminds me of a unit that's deceptive and untrue. Wait! Before I go any further, I'm going to give you law-enforcing liars something you have never given me—and that's a chance to clear the air. No need to thank me, that's only fair. So go ahead—tell me! Aren't you tired of filing false reports, lying as a first resort, and doing the things that you do? If not, you should, because I can't stand the sight of you. I'm tired of hiding behind closed doors, masking my emotions and wallowing in silence when I should be out exploring the world. I'm sick of ignoring the facts, turning the other cheek and smiling while my insides quiver and quarrel. I shouldn't have to pretend, be judged by the color of my skin or have to wait until you to determine the end. I have a right to speak, raise my voice and preach or roam around without being hassled, falsely accused, interrogated or impeached. Therefore, I'm coming out and there's nothing you can do, because God is my Creator and He will see me through! Now you can try to stop me or you can move aside, but I'm coming out—with my head held high! Furthermore, on eggshells, I refuse to walk. Without base, I will never talk. Therefore, why would you think that I would ever confess to doing anything that's not my damn fault? (King James Version, Colossians 1:16)

By Sharon T. Anderson

A Different Kind of Love

I am bold.
I am beautiful.
I am radiant and I am resilient.
I am fierce. I am focused.
I am brawn and I am brilliant.
I am who I am, because I just love being different.

By Sharon T. Anderson

I Stand

Unbiased, I stand and yet, I am often prejudged without reason, criticized, and then condemned, all within a split second and still...I stand.

I stand guilty in the eyes of hatred, as the ongoing sound of malicious echoes damns my very existence and still...I stand.

Not only do I stand to exercise my voice, I stand because I am relevant, I am worthy, and it is my God's given right; therefore, I stand proud! I stand empowered, and I stand with purpose!

Now take heed and stand down, because I do not stand alone. God is with me, and He will never forsake me, for He is a God of His word. With such divine assurance, I stand certain that my prayers will not go unanswered, nor will the impious go unpunished, for God is a true and just God and He sees, hears, and knows all. Therefore, as sure as God is in heaven, the day will come when the righteous rise and the wicked fall. Until then...I stand! (King James Version, Deuteronomy 31:6, King James version, Hebrews 4:13)

By Sharon T. Anderson

A True Warrior

Be not defeated, for you are a warrior...
and warriors always rise!

By Sharon T. Anderson

Left in Darkness

I was left with many unanswered questions and countless concerns, with vague memories and a faint tone. But nothing prepared me for what I was briefly told, for what I was told didn't uphold what I know. So from the elders I looked for truth, but even the elders had no proof. A sudden blanket of silence then covered the land, which obscured my path as it delayed my plans. Still, I refused to give-up or abandon the search, for I'm no quitter or a stranger to work. Therefore, I dug a little deeper and I searched much further and yet, I found nothing. But it was that mysterious feeling of nothingness that led me to believe I was on the verge of finding something great. And with the grace of God, greatness shall rise and darkness will away.

By Sharon T. Anderson

Rise and Shine

Utilize the past to illuminate the present
and the present to secure a much brighter future.

By Sharon T. Anderson

Lost in Emotions

Today, I rose as I have countless times before but somehow, in some peculiar way, today was quite different, and I felt the need to know why. Therefore, in the hopes of finding clarity, question after question, I began asking myself and after hours of intense pondering, the mystery as to why I rose yearning for a love who would never be, for one who displays no interest or desire for me, unfortunately, still remains. Then again, to another my love surely belongs, which makes whatever I am feeling irrelevant and morally wrong, and yet, I sit longing for his presence, for his kind words and his suggestions. Therefore, I ask, "Am I gradually drifting into the forbidden world of darkness, inadvertently becoming a hypocrite or could the root of these sudden and uncontrollable cravings be loneliness and I'm just underestimating its mystical powers?" Whatever the case maybe, I am undeniably lost in emotions and in desperate need of answers. Fortunately, the time for reasoning is in my favor because once this shift finally ends, the same way this mysterious creature drifted into my life, he will then slip out again.

By Sharon T. Anderson

It's Obvious

For some, finding clarity starts with losing the awkward sound of silence,
  while others choose to lose themselves in silence in order to find clarity.
    Whichever you prefer, it's obvious. At some point, we all need clarity.

By Sharon T. Anderson

Undefeated

U...
Undefeated, I shall remain, for not only is the Lord thy
God my savor, He is my pillar, my protector and
my guiding light as well. (Modem English Version, Psalm 18:2–4)

N...
Nothing of this world or of any other could ever stop
me from prevailing because in addition to being a
noble contender, I am and will forever be a
humble and loyal Disciple of Christ.

D...
I am driven by a love that is pure, unparallel and everlasting,
by one of greatness and glory, by a love that is
both definite and divine. I am driven by the word of
my Father, the only son of God, Jesus Christ.
Therefore, I am nothing...if not victorious!

E...
Excellence describes the power from which I graciously
reflect; therefore, with the power vested in me, I
will project nothing less.

F...
Fortitude is an indisputable gift of glory, one of which
I am extremely fortunate to have and will forever
cherish.

E...
Because the Holy Trinity dwells within, I can attest that
most of my battles efficaciously end long before
they ever begin.

A...

In addition to the beautiful blessings listed above, I am
especially grateful for the astounding ability to
remain humble, hopeful and high-spirited
throughout the course of my endeavors.

T...

I stand triumphant, honored and truly blessed to
serve as an anointed Disciple of Christ.

E...

For such empowerment, I attribute all that I am and have
accomplished to the Redeemer, for He is my love,
my light and my salvation.

D...

Father, the gateway to heaven is the very last door that
I wish to enter; therefore, to no other will I ever
bend, beg, bow, serve, or surrender. Amen

By Sharon T. Anderson

Rebuke, Maintain, and Rejoice

Do not let your weaknesses overpower your strengths, your fears overshadow your confidence or be misled by false prophets and their fictitious predictions. Do not let sorrow replace your joy, anxiousness disrupt your peace or allow yourself to fall in the hands of the wicked. However, most importantly, do not let the enemy slither in and take what is rightfully yours, because in the sight of those who believe, stands a divine warrior of God, a man of faith, courage, compassion, wisdom, conviction and might. Therefore, maintain an optimistic attitude and continue utilizing your God given gifts to confuse and defeat your opponents. Furthermore, with the help of Our Father, you will prevail so bow your head and prepare to rejoice!

By Sharon T. Anderson

I Surrender

I...
I crave a life that no other can provide, O Lord...a life
that's definite and divine, of love and loyalty, one
that's surrounded by peace, compassion, consistency
and kindness. I long for a life that's beautiful,
vibrant, happy and healthy. But most of all, I yearn
for an everlasting life in the kingdom of heaven.

S...
So, until this life is over and you deem me worthy for the
next, I will serve, I will sacrifice, I will bend and I
will bow, and I will do everything within my power
to fulfill my obligations as a Disciple of Christ.

U...
Use me as you will, O Lord, for I am yours...now and forever.

R...
Remove these self-imposed shackles and give me the
courage to rise, the power to rule, and the sense to
remain rational.

R...
Reveal the intentions of the opposition and let victory
reign in my favor, for not only am I ready to face the
enemy, I am prepared to defeat the enemy!

E...
Empower me to transform the depraved into disciples,
adversaries into allies, and the grounds on which we
battle into a place of everlasting peace, compassion and harmony.

N...

Now is the time to uplift, instill, nurture and provide.
It's time for the faithful to join forces, become
mentors and take the lead. The time has come for us
to educate, advise, prepare and guide. But most
importantly, now is the time to raise a nation that's diligent,
devoted, determined and divine. Therefore, in
order to succeed, O Lord, the gift of wisdom
is what I humbly beg of thee.

D...

Despite life's challenges, I pledge to remain earnest,
optimistic and dedicated, especially in times of
darkness, desperation, and despair.

E...

Examine my mind, my body and my soul for repressed
emotions, feelings of resentment and negativity, O
Lord, and then I ask that you enable me to emit such
findings with integrity, serenity and grace.

R...

Revive me, O Lord...for I cannot do this alone. Amen.

By Sharon T. Anderson

In God's Hands

Let the weight of the world rest in God's hands
and stress-free, you will forever stand.
(King James Version, Matt. 11:28–30)

By Sharon T. Anderson

The Appetite to Succeed

Father, I am here kneeling before you yet again,
because I don't know how to get started
or where to begin. So I'm going to start from the
top…and I'll let you determine the end.
I was once well-known for being ambitious,
stupendous, vibrant and alive. However, I
am now popular for dragging my feet and
wasting time. Lord, I don't know what
happened or where I went wrong but somehow,
I have fallen into the comfort zone.
Therefore, I beg you to give me the courage to
face my fears and the energy to strive,
because I am tired of watching from the sidelines.
God, you are my only hope, you're my
inspiration, and you are the only true commander
and chief. Therefore, I am asking you
to bless me with the willpower to keep moving
forward, and the appetite to succeed.
(King James Version, 1 Timothy 1:15)

By Sharon T. Anderson

Stop letting
Procrastination
Impede
Your
Path!

By Sharon T. Anderson

Heavenly Father, in addition to the glorious gift of life,

I graciously thank thee for a life of **I**nfinite love,

for a love that's indisputably **A**wesome, absolute, and

100 percent authentic, for one that's **M**erciful, magnificent, miraculous and divine. But most of all, I thank thee, O Lord, for being the love of my lifeline! (King James Version, Ephesians 2:4–10)

By Sharon T. Anderson

Forever Grateful

Heavenly Father, I am either kneeling before thee with a heavy heart or I am calling with countless requests, but rarely do I give proper thanks and for that, I am utterly ashamed. Therefore, I graciously thank you for every mystical moment, O Lord. I thank you for the ravishing rainbows and the bountiful blessings, as well as the lows, the woes and life's indelible lessons, because if it had not been for such tribulations, I would probably be incapable of showing a hint appreciation. Furthermore, until the clock stops ticking and time stands still, I will forever give thanks as in your will. Amen

By Sharon T. Anderson

Sudden Change

Shortly after I began traveling down this winding road,
    I discovered a few things I didn't know.

Some things were good, and some were bad.
    In addition to feeling happy, I felt terribly sad.

So I fell to my knees and I began to pray,
    that God uplifts my spirit and brightens my day.

Suddenly, the weather changed and the sun popped out,
    so I grabbed my tambourine and I began to shout!

Joy filled my heart like never before,
    then the music stopped and I heard a roar.

Seconds later, there was a boom and then a bang!
    Therefore, I took cover to escape the rain.

But I couldn't stay, I was forced out by the birds and the bees,
    and the voices of the trees.

However, I could have refused or put up a fight but instead,
    I began running through the meadows like a thief in the night.

I'm currently resting on a different plain.
    However, I will always expect that sudden change!

By Sharon T. Anderson

Initiate Change

Stop blaming everyone else when there is no one to blame except yourself, because mistakes will happen as they often do, but if you crave change, it must start with you!

By Sharon T. Anderson

Alphabet Soup

Like many others, I have good days and I have bad days. Therefore, whenever I become overwhelmed, have a meltdown or experience a lack of enthusiasm, I take a five-minute breather. Not only do I utilize this time to collect my thoughts, it gives me a chance to empower my mind with a double dose of alphabet soup…and it's far from ordinary. In fact, it's beyond compare. However, there is one catch. The reader must chant with conviction and might. In other words, he/she must believe.

I'm: **A**mbitious
      Loyal and **L**ovable
      Patient and **P**roficient
      Hopeful
      Articulate and **A**ssertive
      Bold and **B**eautiful
      Efficient and **E**ager
      Tenacious and **T**alented

I'm: **S**tupendous and **S**tudious
      Optimistic and **O**pen-minded
      Unique and **U**nforgettable
      Professional and **P**assionate

It does not matter if its work related or personal, the next time you need a quick stress reliever or a boost of confidence, try consuming a little **alphabet soup.**

By Sharon T. Anderson

Be Inspired

Becoming something starts with stopping at nothing!

By Sharon T. Anderson

Sacred Jewels

By an elder, I was once told to treasure the heirlooms of glitter and gold. Bless each piece before passing them along, and then watch the bond between generations grow divinely strong. Together, you shall rise after this deed is done, but your name shall ring for generations to come. However, there's a tiny twist to this age-old tale, so open your ears and listen well. If the bond is broken during the first initial quest, even the victories of your ancestors will be laid to rest. So wear these jewels proudly and keep them safe, for the victory of your own empire depends on faith.

By Sharon T. Anderson

Beacon of Hope

I can hear the voices of my second, third, and fourth child,
 but I haven't heard a peep out of my first in a while.

It seems like he's a stationed million miles away,
 even though both of us reside in the very same state.

Maybe I'm too sensitive or maybe paranoia is to blame. Maybe it's
 time to stop pointing fingers and start focusing on a positive
 plan of change.

So until this is over and my son is back where he belongs,
 I'm going to do everything within my power to bring my son
 back home.

I was told to stop dreaming and let nature take its course,
 but that would make me a failure, a failure with lots of
 remorse.

Perhaps I'm an optimist and striving is the way I cope,
 so why would I ever stop striving when there's always a beacon
 of hope?

By Sharon T. Anderson

Deception

Would you deem one worthy based on sight and sound alone? It is unfortunate but more often than not, many make the mistake of confiding in deceptive appearing saints instead of faithfully entrusting in the Lord. For such carelessness, most subjects find themselves under sudden attack and/or miserably failing and they have little or no clue as to why, which usually make matters much worse. I say this because the work of adversaries are best done in the dark but when the truth finally becomes known, the enemy stands as a person who you would least expect 99 percent of the time and he/she is normally a close relative, a lover or a friend. Therefore, stop taking chances on those who appear soulful and start calling on the Lord, because not only is He available 24-7, He will never lead you astray!

By Sharon T. Anderson

from honor, stems **L**oyalty
in loyalty, there is **O**rder
order **Y**ields trust
trust mirrors **A**ssurance
assurance instills **L**ight
and light emits **T**ranquility,
but it all starts with **Y**ou

By Sharon T. Anderson

Inquiring Minds

When did this happen?
How can it be?
Where were you going?
Were you that intrigued?
Why did you flee,
then deliberately lie?
Were you foolishly focused,
or bogusly blind?
I refuse push, nor will I pry.
But these are questions of inquiring minds!

By Sharon T. Anderson

The Last Word

Sometimes, the last word can be one word too
many, because it has the power to
determine the beginning as well as the end, so be mindful.

By Sharon T. Anderson

Control Free

Warning…you have just entered a control free zone; therefore, thoroughly review the following terms and conditions and if you concur, proceed with extreme caution. Otherwise, immediately exit the premises.

0. The amount of tolerance I have for those who project negativity is zero; therefore, it is strictly forbidden.
1. There shall be no using, abusing or misusing.
2. Refrain from playing manipulating mind games.
3. Pull your weight. Do not become the weight.
4. Honor your word, without turning your word into a war of words.
5. Maintain an open and honest line of communication.
6. Never assume, falsely accuse or act as if you're the one exception to the rule.
7. Respect the feelings, the wishes and the property of others.
8. Ask not, take not.
9. Nothings permanent, so know your place.
10. Above all, put God first! (The Living Bible, Proverbs 3–6)

By Sharon T. Anderson

It Takes Two

I am no expert, nor do I pretend to be.
> However, when it comes to giving advice, that's my area of expertise.

I'm also old-fashioned and I have old-fashioned ways,
> but don't think for a second you have a live-in maid.

So try to be understanding, because understanding is the key.
> Therefore, start lending a helping hand; otherwise, you'll be forced to leave.

Or maybe I am just too blind, too blind to see...
> how much of a jerk you really are to me.

So listen carefully, because I refuse to repeat this twice.
> It takes two, two to do things right.

By Sharon T. Anderson

Slackers

I'm not here to judge or criticize.
I'm not here to dictate or supervise.
I'm not here to point fingers, call names or throw
darts because if you're a slacker, you
know who you are.

So don't try to deny it, make excuses or fight it.
Don't try to avoid me or start ignoring me.
Please, don't change the subject, shy away or
start acting bizarre because as you know,
slackers never get far.

Now that you know where I stand, let's establish
some rules…because I'm trying to
prevent myself from overheating or blowing a fuse.
Pull your weight and I'll pull mines.
And at the end of the day, we'll still be fine!

By Sharon T. Anderson

A Special Blend

Are you tired of being frowned upon, talked about and laughed at? Do you need a different approach, a new outlook or a change in attitude? If so, try my very own special blend of suggestions! First, grab a bowl of belief. Then add four cups of faith, three sticks of charisma, two tablespoons of optimism, 1 slice of love, plenty of patience, lots of laughter, a cube of kindness, a ton of attentiveness, and a generous amount of compassion. For twice as much zest, whisk in a pound of all-purpose pizzazz, some extra strength etiquette, a splash of caliente, an hour of warmth, a dash of joy and an ounce of intelligence. Second, shake well and then consume. Finally yet importantly, chase my special blend of suggestions down with an eight-ounce glass of strength. Because after ingesting a potion this potent, you will instantly see and feel a remarkable change. Therefore, bottoms up...and congratulations. You are now on your way to a better you!

By Sharon T. Anderson

Diversely Unique

Ladies, regardless of our differences, it's a fact that each one of us enjoys having our egos stroked in one way or the other. And as long as it goes uninterrupted, everything appears perfectly aligned and beautifully balanced. However, once those blissful moments end, either our guards go up and the claws come out or the analyzing, the comparing and the complaining begin. Whatever the case may be, ladies, we spend an excessive amount of time complaining about our imperfections, our wants, our needs, and sometimes, our innermost desires. More often than not, we even seem to fuss about things we occasionally miss but seldom lack. Face it…we are all different in spirit and appearance. Therefore, let's stop dwelling on what we don't have, could have and should have, and start praising God for the many things we do have…because if He wanted all women to look the same, act the same and think the same, we would all be the same and that would leave no room for diversity or change. Simply put, none of us would ever feel incredibly beautiful or diversely unique if we were all perky and petite with a perfectly formed physique.

By Sharon T. Anderson

Triple A

Thanks to genetics, I am indisputably
Awesome, **A**bsolute and 100 percent **A**uthentic

By Sharon T. Anderson

Just Listen

Shh! Don't talk, just listen! I've been diagnosed
with a very rare yet uncontrollable
condition. So take a few steps back and maintain
a safe distance, unless you've been
medically cleared by a licensed physician.

Stop! At least wait until you've heard the underlying
symptom before you start acting
bizarre or going ballistic. It's not what you think.
You're the culprit and I'm the victim.
Therefore, close your mouth, take a sit and
please…just listen. Because somehow,
I knew this would get your undivided attention.

Like the wings of a hummingbird or the buzzing
of a bee, my heart still flutters whenever
you're near me. I didn't think it was possible
until I laid eyes on you, then my world
changed from gray to blue. Based on your reaction,
I don't know if you consider this as
being good but I'm certain it's not bad. So let's
resolve our differences and rekindle the
love we've once had.

By Sharon T. Anderson

Memorable Moments

Although I've been blessed with a lifetime of
memorable moments, not one warms my
heart like the second I laid eyes on you.

By Sharon T. Anderson

For Once

For once, I wanna push my fears aside, swallow my pride and then go take a walk on the wild side. I wanna live carefree, go on a shopping spree and indulge without harboring the guilt of not counting those annoying calories. I wanna misbehave, stay gone for days and then return like I've been overworked but well paid. I wanna dress more provocative, be less cooperative and let the world know that it's solely my prerogative.

For once, I wanna leave my worries behind, sleep until nine and then rise to the chilling taste of America's finest wine. I wanna stumble when I walk, babble when I talk and then pocket a few tips without being caught. I wanna forget about dignity, vent with hostility and explore the world without having an ounce of responsibility. I wanna travel in style, chill out awhile and then I wanna use my professional assets to alter my personal profile.

For once, I wanna twerk before a crowd, walk away with a smile and then turn around and laugh out loud. I wanna roast all night, deliberately start a fight and then accuse my opponent of being obnoxiously uptight. I wanna be the baddest chick, check the neighborhood snitch and then walk around like I'm legit. I wanna take them down hard, laugh from afar and then I wanna go party like a rock star!

For once, I just wanna walk away…and let my alter ego take charge.

By Sharon T. Anderson

Seize the Moment

When words go unspoken, the moment is lost
and the opportunity fades, doubt is evoked
and questions are raised. So do not hold back,
stand up, and give it your all, for there is
nothing more powerful than a heart of gumption and gall.

By Sharon T. Anderson

Fifty Fabulous Years

Here's a play-by-play of the first fifty days after my fiftieth birthday. I forwarded all calls, visited the local malls, embraced Hawaiians style, strolled with a smile, got a massage, overtipped just because, painted the town red, chillaxed on chocolate-covered bed, rose with the sun, sunbathed on the beach, ingested several drinks, exceeded the legal peak, bypassed cloud nine, reserved time to dine, grabbed a grass skirt, vivaciously began to flirt, established a connection, enjoyed the affection, laid under the stars, and then I got up and partied to no other than Bruno Mars. Furthermore, I consumed lots of pork, pigged out without a fork, took a last-minute cruise, inhaled additional booze, felt extremely queasy, tried to take it easy, popped twenty Tums, chased them with rum, fell into the aisle, laid for a while, crawled through the leaves, stumbled to my knees, sat on a bench, regained a hint of strength, laughed out loud, immediately drew a crowd, cracked a few jokes, laughed at the jokes they poked, slowly saved face and continued to acknowledge God's glorious grace. I also rented a cabana, planned a sequel in Santa Anna, glanced at the check, changed the subject, sampled something smoky, rocked the karaoke, rolled with the waves, surfed as I prayed, swam back to shore, felt awfully sore, summoned a masseuse, went from tight to loose, and then I tried some coconut flavored Kahlua and I wished I had tried it much soona. In addition to that, I created floral banners, joined the hula dancers, gracefully moved my feet, mirrored the natives beats and just praised God Almighty…for the fifty fabulous years that He has granted me.

By Sharon T. Anderson

A Diabetics Delight

Don't call me reckless or noncompliant,
    just because I'm a disbeliever of medicine and science!

I'm a free spirit, which means, I have no limitations.
    Therefore, I will never follow guidelines or eat in moderation.

Instead, prescribe a plan of immeasurable pleasure,
    because I'm not interested in pamphlets, sermons or diabetic
    lectures.

I want biscuits, bacon, cakes and pies…
    linguine, lasagna, lobster, and fries.

I want pizza, pasta, giblets and gravy.
    I want a course that's outrageously tasty!

So exclude the lettuce and omit the tomatoes,
    take away the celery and then add a potato.

Remember the peppers, the chives and the cheese,
    for I want flavor…not a tease.

By Sharon T. Anderson

Mr. Sandman

Dear Mr. Sandman,

Night after night, I toss and I turn as I wait for you to come along. You are never on time, and you find humor in being late. But to me, there is nothing humorous about falling asleep moments before I am scheduled to awake! I'm sure you're helping another unwind, but you have been running behind for quite some time. Therefore, this might sound a little harsh or completely rude, so how you perceive this message depends on you. Sir, please save your siestas for the younger crowd, because I am tired of waking up feeling down. And if you really are the sovereign of sleep, clear your schedule and prepare to meet. I'm demanding an explanation of why you're deliberately depriving me of sleep!

Sincerely yours,
Sharon T. Anderson

A Day of Rest

I'm reserving this day for a day of rest.
Therefore, I will not cook.
I will not clean.
I refuse to yell, nor will I scream.
So for the time being, I'm going to step aside
and let you do your own thing.

By Sharon T. Anderson

From Beginning to End

In the beginning, our love conquered all. There were no mistakes, no secretes, no jealously or flaws. We were impeccable, joint at the hip and inseparable. We stood side by side, found comfort and took pride. It didn't matter if you had less or if I had more, because you were my crutch as I was yours.

Now you're very distant and cold, ruthless and bold. Negativity moves you. It reels you in and then it consumes you. And when it comes to priorities, I'm sorry but you have none. Because running wild…is far from living or having fun. Therefore, for whatever your reason or explanation may be, it's clear there is definitely no unity.

However, although my love remains unchanged, I refuse to undergo another day of heartache and pain. In agony is not where I want to be. Therefore, wipe your eyes, step aside and set me free. Exploring the world is what I intend to do, and my plans of adventure does not include you. I'm sorry…but this is where it has to end. So walk away, grit your teeth, and try to grin!

By Sharon T. Anderson

Accept the Facts

The truth has already been revealed;
therefore, open your eyes and accept the facts!

By Sharon T. Anderson

Undeniably Irresistible

Ladies, if nothing else, I am sure that most of us have had the pleasure of secretly meeting with "Dr. Feel Good" on more than one occasion. Therefore, I will not bore you with redundant details, nor will I add to the circulation of rumors that initially aroused my curiosity years ago. However, in the hopes of preventing future prospects from making similar mistakes, I will undoubtedly shower each one with great words of continuous wisdom. Besides, it takes somewhat of an expert to confront, forewarn and enlighten newcomers about the history and unconventional habits of "The Good Dr.," without expressing a hint of resentment. Therefore, whenever the opportunity presents itself, instead of seizing the chance to rain on his parade, ladies, take the opportunity to educate the inexperienced about the risks, the consequences and the potential dangers of having work-related affairs. After all, it's no secret that a vast number of both men and women consider the workplace as being the perfect playground away from home, and he/she will do almost anything to have his/her wild oats sewn and frankly, we are no exception, so don't you think the clueless has a right to know?

Then again, work-related affairs will continue regardless, but at least the inquisitive will have the knowledge to proceed with his/her eyes wide open. Now, for those who don't quite understand, allow me to elaborate or better yet, put this into laymen terms. Heartbreakers exist and they will go on existing in every organization, in every city and in every nation and fortunately, the average one stick out like a sore thumb. Then, there are those who you would least expect, those who master the game and unfortunately, heartbreakers of this breed possess qualities that are nothing less than magnetic, which makes the process of befriending new targets seem rather effortless. Ladies, now that you have a clear understanding of how these highly skilled players acquired their title (Dr. Feel Good), let's focus on the game (Catch and Release) that's sending most of their victims into a sudden state of confusion. With that said, put your thinking caps on and read between the lines, because the name (Catch and Release) alone speaks for itself, and since time is of the essence, it would be foolish to waste it on anything that's self-explanatory; however, this is how the game works.

Prior to orientation, "Dr. Feel Good" spends a considerable amount of time plotting, planning and anxiously waiting for the next fresh, yet distinctive aroma of new arrivals. The day of, he locks in a target and proceeds to greet the subject as he would any other. This is primarily done for two reasons: it gives "The Good Dr." a chance to show the person of interest that he's approachable and second, it allows him to determine the target's level of vulnerability. He then allows a few days to past before initiating a quick conversation of small talk and if all goes well, "Catch and Release" officially begins. Until now, "Catch and Release" sounds harmless but unfortunately, it's far from. The subject has no idea that he/she is under attack, which leaves him/her defenseless and open for fire. The next three steps (earning trust, brainwashing, isolating) are also no-brainers; therefore, I'm going to fast forward to the fourth and final step. Ladies, by now, you should already know what that entails. It should also be obvious that once the chase or challenge ends, so does the relationship and "The Good Dr." is off and running, only to repeat the process elsewhere...so beware.

In closing, heartbreakers are universal and not only do they come in all nationalities, shapes and sizes, the sex of these smooth operators can be of either gender, which many fail to realize. For that reason, female players frequently go overlooked, are underestimated and in some instances, the games in which they play go undetected altogether. Finally and most importantly, manipulators often succeed because we simply assume. And as you know, assumption is the cause of most preventable mishaps; therefore, if you do not want to become the latest victim of "Catch and Release," stop ignoring the signs, ask relevant questions and start reading between the lines.

By Sharon T. Anderson

Never Turn a Blind Eye

Although many of us long for a life of everlasting
clarity, some find it easier to turn a
blind eye instead of facing the facts, especially
when it comes to love and relationships.
Perhaps love is to blame for these bogus and
selfless acts or maybe, it's something far
more complex. In any case, masking your
emotions are not only misleading, it's
exhausting, unhealthy and hurtful. Therefore,
why waste time harboring ill feelings when
true happiness awaits?

By Sharon T. Anderson

Man Up!

Wake up, my sistahs…look around and then tell me what you see! I see brothas of all nationalities preying on articulate sistahs like me. By no means am I saying that all men are the same. I'm just tired of listening to brothas sell females dreams of glitz, glamour and fame. Now don't get me wrong, because I'm a team player when it comes to helping anyone that's ambitiously strong. But, there is a difference between lending a helping hand and literally supporting a fraud… with a plan. Therefore, fellas, for those of you who think I'm just another come up, I suggest you grow some balls and man up! Face it…I will never be a cash out, become a puppet on a string or a sellout. So for once, take responsibility and stop looking for damn handouts!

By Sharon T. Anderson

Seriously

If not words of **substance**,
security or **solidarity**,
save that pillow talk for one night stands!

By Sharon T. Anderson

Holiday Ho's

The holidays are here again,
and the urge to give is stirring within.

I have one chance to do this right.
Therefore, I plan to appear on Christmas night.

I'm sure this will be a memorable surprise,
especially for those with wondering eyes.

So join me under the mistletoe,
and let's jump-start the New Year…with a ho, ho, ho!

By Sharon T. Anderson

Overheated Holidays

Father Time...thanks for cursing me with glaucoma, poor vision and bifocals because without those ailments, I'm sure it would be virtually impossible for me to see the **New Year** with clarity and cheer.

Cupid, cancel my subscription and then cross me off the list because every **Valentine's Day**. you try mending my broken heart with nothing more than a measly candy coated kiss instead of sending lots of love or granting my wish.

Mr. Cottontail... although I did not feel the need to unwind, I have experienced a loss of consciousness over a dozen times. Therefore, where do you find the strength to remain conscious during the constant cracking of those smelly hard-boiled eggs several days after **Easter**?

I would like to give the fire marshal five stars for lighting my pilot, keeping it well lit, and then for gradually putting out my **Fourth of July** flames, without boring me the details or even asking my name.

Thanks to the misdiagnosis of the orthodontist, I now have just enough teeth to discourage heavy snackers from consuming those **Sweetest Day** treats.

Haters, I'm coming out to personally show you how grateful I am for forcing me to reveal my true identity on the one day of the year that it's actually acceptable so beware, because I'll be the one dressed as the typical **Halloween** witch!

Thanks to the holiday hustlers, the pint-sized pimps and the jive turkeys that are completely flooding street, I no longer desire **Thanksgiving** turkey or any other unsavory pieces of meat!

Santa, I hate to rain on your parade or drag your mythical sleigh in the shade, but don't you think it's time to retire that big red robe, dim the light on Rudolph's bright red nose and come clean? If you don't, I do! Therefore, have your tiny green men in those tightly curled shoes to fetch Mrs. Clause so she can break the news! Better yet, forget the runners. It's my pitch, so I'll do the honors! Now that I have you all packed in one room, here's a riddle of a different tune. So hold your questions until the end or inquire before I begin. Anyway, for centuries, parents have been bending over backwards, depleting their savings and robbing Peter just to pay Paul in order to shower their loved ones with gifts of continuous joy and yet, they rarely receive simple thanks. Instead, trillions glorify your name before, during and even after the holiday season, Santa. For the reasons stated above, I hereby strip you of your seasonal rights…so stay off the radar during the eve of **Christmas** night!

By Sharon T. Anderson

Faithful Friend

F...is for being <u>faithful</u> and true.
  A...represents an <u>admirable</u> view.
    I...stands for the <u>inspiration</u> you instill each day.
      T...signifies you're <u>trustworthy</u> in every way.
        H...displays a person of <u>honesty</u> and hope.
          F...proves you're <u>forgiving</u> when I'm unable to cope.
            U...are an angel when it comes to <u>understanding</u> and belief.
            L...ensures the <u>loyalty</u> you have for me.

F...explains how fortunate I am to have you as a <u>friend</u>.
  R...<u>releases</u> the love within.
    I...is for being <u>informative</u> and wise.
      E...<u>exhibits</u> a person that's genuinely kind.
        N...narrows it down to strength, courage and <u>nobility</u>
          D...<u>delivers</u> a world of everlasting tranquility.

By Sharon T. Anderson

Nothing but Trash

Stop! There shall be no more pretending,
    for I'm sure by now you know the ending.

You are not who you pretend to be.
    I'm just sorry I let you happen to me.

So, back to the gutter you shall go,
    along with the lies that you call hope.

And I'll refrain from calling you a loss,
    since recycled trash clearly cost.

Still, it's my fault and for that, I'm grossly ashamed,
    for I only have me, myself, and I to blame.

Thus, from this day forward, instead of picking up garbage, I'll be
    saving myself for the open, the honest and the kind hearted.

By Sharon T. Anderson

Clear Your Conscience

I am no psychic; however, I can sense when there is something wrong, and I have been sensing something wrong for far too long. Therefore, you can clear your conscience by telling me what's on your mind, because I am fed up with trying to read between the lines! You sound convincing, but your actions speaks louder than words. So toughen up…and let the truth be heard. If you will not confide in me, at least bow your head and kneel before Christ, because He has the power… the power to make it all right.

By Sharon T. Anderson

Forgiveness

Remember friend, forgiveness is the key.
You want my forgiveness, so why won't you really forgive me?

You've said that I'm forgiven, but that's entirely not true.
Because if u really meant it, I wouldn't feel the way I do.

Forgiveness involves more than just the sound of spoken words.
It's an action, it's a feeling, and it's the one thing I deserve!

You have my forgiveness, now please set me free.
Otherwise, you'll forever be a prisoner…of misery.

By Sharon T. Anderson

Suggestive Opportunities

Opportunities come and opportunities go,
but will opportunities wait? Hell no!

So take advantage whenever you can,
for great opportunities will wait on no man.

Furthermore, if you are not serious or at least prepping,
opportunities suggest that you keep on stepping.

By Sharon T. Anderson

Up Your Game

Look! Haters will hate regardless. Therefore,
never lower your standards just to fit in or
to impress. Instead, up your game and let haters
wallow in their own abominable mess.

By Sharon T. Anderson

Have Faith

H...<u>Have</u> faith, for the Lord thy God is truly worthy (King James
Version, Rev. 4:11)
    A...<u>apply</u> yourself, never deny yourself
        V...<u>Venture</u> out, dismiss the doubt
            E...<u>Explore</u>, eliminate, and then select

F...<u>Focus</u> on the greater good
    A...<u>Aim</u> for the stars; however, shoot to exceed
        I...<u>Invest</u> in yourself and invest wisely
            T...<u>Trust</u> your instincts and never stop believing
                H...<u>Honor</u> your word with respect and dignity

By Sharon T. Anderson

Payday

I still look forward to payday,
  although it's no fun getting paid.
   My pay is a joke.
    I'm always broke,
     and what money I have seems to fade.

I still look forward to payday.
  However, now, I refuse to complain…
   for God is in charge.
    He knows my heart,
     and I still have His trust to gain.

I still look forward to payday.
  Only now, I can't wait to get paid.
   My future appears bright.
    My energy is high,
     and my Father keeps me amazed.

By Sharon T. Anderson

In Good Faith, it was given; therefore, return it without fuss, frowns and in full, for payment plans are unacceptable!

By Sharon T. Anderson

Secrets

Secrets are never safe, well-kept or simply forgotten.
Instead, they are temporarily stored in the memory
banks of the vindictive, the ruthless
and the rotten. Therefore, the next time you think
your secret is safe, keep this in mind.
The walls have ears, the sky has eyes, and secrets
never remain safe for more than just a
brief period of time.

By Sharon T. Anderson

World Peace

If I could, I would sit among the stars overlooking
the sea, and bask in a world of
everlasting serenity. I would travel from coast-to-
coast emitting light both high and low
until the hearts of the world felt nothing
other than joy, peace, love and hope.

If I could, I would give observers a nighttime
surprise of shooting stars that's on the rise.
And on those cold dreary nights when Mother
Nature appears a little bitter and uptight, I
would burn extra long and shine twice as bright.

If I could, I would rid the world of those godforsaken
woes, soothe the weary, add a layer
of comfort and then off to the land of dreams
humanity would doze. However, for every
heartfelt wish addressed to me, the hopeful would
rest on the coziest clouds of harmony.

If I could, I would transform those unsettling
feelings of ill will into acts of kindness,
peace and goodwill. But most importantly, the
world would finally be in a state of
absolute bliss, because those tension producing
problems would cease exist.

By Sharon T. Anderson

Guardian of Peace

I will let nothing disrupt my peace because
without peace, there is misery and misery
craves the company I refuse to keep!

By Sharon T. Anderson

The Wings of Freedom

In the wings of an angel, I rest weightless and free,
    free from stress, free from burden and free from agony.

Beyond the clouds and through the stars my soul shall soar…
    to a heavenly place where trumpets of gold roar.

There will be no weeping for what I have once endured,
    for I'll finally be swaddled in a love that's pure.

So don't fret, make a fuss or shed one tear,
    cause my soul longs for the one whom I love so dear.

By Sharon T. Anderson

I Need

Everyone loves extra padding, especially in the pocket; however, not everyone will work for the cause. With that said, if you are among those who fit the above description, under no circumstances should you ever approach me while expelling the following words, "I need." Furthermore, if you want it, work for it and stop shifting your weight or weighing others down, trying to get it!

By Sharon T. Anderson

Why seek support
if you're not willing **sacrifice**?

By Sharon T. Anderson

Unbreakable

I am a born believer, a follower of faith, and one divine disciple as well. Therefore, I am of greatness and glory. However, make no mistake, for I will bend, but I will never break!

By Sharon T. Anderson

Never underestimate the power of a woman,
especially if she's your source of **POWER!**

By Sharon T. Anderson

Driven by Faith

Heavenly Father, I will forever glorify your
holy name, for it is the faith I
have in you that keeps me focused, well
fueled, and graciously moving
forward.

By Sharon T. Anderson

Focus with faith,
    for *faith never fails*.

By Sharon T. Anderson

A Dreamer's Reality

I would not ordinarily tell anyone to stop
dreaming, because most success stories start
with an amazing dream. **However, it takes more
than a dream to become successful**.
Therefore, how long are you going to stay tightly
tucked in bed before you decide turn
fantasy into reality?

By Sharon T. Anderson

Wake Up!

By Sharon T. Anderson

Soulful Sentiments

It's unfortunate but not all sentiments are soulful, especially when they come from the mouths of those who find pleasure in criticizing or dampening the spirits of others. They are far from sincere when one openly sniggers at another's downfall, nor are they heartfelt when a confidant displays pure disgust as his/her companion becomes successful. Sentiments are not exactly soulful when those who gain trust disclose intimate secretes and partake in harmful gossip. However, nothing disturbs me more than those who stand before the righteous, with words of kindness while secretly harboring ill feelings. Frenemies of this sort are much harder to detect unless they inadvertently reveal themselves. However, do not fret, for God has a divine way of exposing all darkness! He has a way of removing every impediment, every obstacle and every stumbling block; therefore, give it to God and let Him lighten the load. Then sit back and watch how the King transforms those very same frenemies into two legged footstools!

By Sharon T. Anderson

Back to Basics

Focus with faith and soar in silence; otherwise,
you're doing nothing more than giving the
opposition ammunition to fire before takeoff.

By Sharon T. Anderson

Self-Worth

Love can be beautiful, slightly complex or a complete and utter disaster. In any case, one should never underestimate its mystical powers, because not only is it responsible for holding love-stricken individuals hostage, it is to blame for most of their choices, their actions and their unfortunate mishaps. For the previously stated reasons, many subjects see, hear and do what they want regardless of the highflying red flags and continuous words of warnings. In fact, some even have the audacity to overlook the obvious even when it's clearly in plain sight. Maybe it's the idea of being in love that is keeping these individuals so tightly bound or perhaps, it's the petrifying notion of possibly growing old alone. Although there seems to be countless excuses, not one justifies or gives a logical explanation of why love-stricken individuals remain in hopeless relationships. Not one clarifies why most subjects have tendencies of loving and respecting their mates more than they actually love and respect themselves. With that said, I have come to realize that this mind-boggling mystery may very well go unresolved; therefore, I will conclude with a few words of wisdom. Everyone deserves a life of hope, harmony and happiness, so until true love presents itself, stop wasting valuable time on worthless prospects and know that you are priceless!

By Sharon T. Anderson

If it's not uplifting, it's a
weight that needs releasing.
Let go and allow yourself to **rise!**

By Sharon T. Anderson

Under Armor

Satan! You've tried getting up close and personal. You've even tried attacking from afar. But your tactics are indisputably useless, because I know who and what you really are. So fall back, stand down, or face me like a man. For not only does the blood of Jesus covers me, my fate lies within God's hands. Now that you know I am **under armor**, I command you to flee! My soul belongs to the Creator. Therefore, you have no rights to me!

By Sharon T. Anderson

You are not alone.
I AM Forever Present!

By Sharon T. Anderson

For most, revenge is the quickest way to instant gratification; however, **be not tempted**,

for vengeance is not yours to seek. It belongs to the Lord and in due time,

not only will the guilty be held accountable; they will indisputably feel the great Wrath of

God. Until then, let nothing harden your heart, dwell in peace and remain humble. (King James Version, Romans 12:17–19)

By Sharon T. Anderson

It's All About

J
Include **E** Flourish
S
Exclude **U** Fail
S

By Sharon T. Anderson

I am only accepting **vivacious vibes**. Therefore, I have zero room for gloom and negativity is an absolute no, no!

By Sharon T. Anderson

Beautiful Bonds

Respectful
Encouraging
Loving
Affectionate
Trustworthy
Inspirational
Optimistic
Nurturing
Sincere
Heartwarming
Insightful
Passionate

Are Never Broken

By Sharon T. Anderson

Words of Wisdom

If someone/something causes more pain than
pleasure, sever all ties and seriously let go
because obviously, the subject is more of a hindrance than a helper.

By Sharon T. Anderson

If it's not clean, it's cluttered.
Make Room!

By Sharon T. Anderson

The Perfect Remedy

Sometimes you just have to
ignore the ignorant and
bypass the bullshit in order
to get where you need to go!

By Sharon T. Anderson

Food for Thought

It's impossible to make a touchdown if you never tap in.

By Sharon T. Anderson

C4

It is not your responsibility to bear the burdens of others, nor do you possess the strength to carry the weight of the world. Therefore, the following may sound a bit harsh and can even be quite difficult but every now and again, everyone should C4 (cross out, declutter, reconfigure, and then mentally, physically, and spiritually cleanse) in order to unwind and completely decompress.

By Sharon T. Anderson

Distance yourself from darkness.

Live within light.

Prepare for everlasting peace.

By Sharon T. Anderson

The Bigger Picture

Life is a gift that comes with many valuable lessons and with each lesson is the opportunity to learn. However, when a subject fails to take heed after making the same countless mistakes, are you quick to criticize, prejudge or pass judgment without proven facts or are you a person of compassion, one who are not only willing to lend a helping hand, but who will also tackle any task regardless of size? Such questions play a major role in improving self-awareness because although most consider themselves exceptional role models, there is nothing exceptional about jumping to conclusions, speculating or assuming the worst. Furthermore, not everyone is glutton for punishment or trying to escape the responsibilities of work. Many struggle with learning disabilities, disorders and debilitating diseases. Because of such, most are too afraid and/ashamed to seek assistance while others find it much easier to simply shy away. With that said, imagine what the above individuals undergo within a single day, self-adjust if possible and then reveal your findings. Unfortunately, the outcome is a no-brainer, because the majority of participants would not know where to begin or how to cope. Therefore, make your next encounter an optimistic experience, especially for those who need it the most. Above all else, stop focusing on every minute detail and start concentrating on the bigger picture.

By Sharon T. Anderson

Make every moment **memorable.**

Make it **remarkable.**

Make it **count.**

By Sharon T. Anderson

Beautifully Balanced

My family is nowhere near perfect but then again, what family is? Like any other, we have our differences and more often than not, they are far from sound. However, those same dissimilarities make us quite vivacious, especially during seasonal gatherings and family functions. Even on the Sabbath day, the day of peace, order and accordance, we face challenges. For instance, a few may stroll into the house of the Lord hours late and nearly bare while others are forever prompt and properly dressed. As most add to the collection plate, one or two may possibly take from the plate of offerings. Then, there are those who are undeniably popular for clowning around, joking and dancing through the aisles during the most inopportune time. To observers, my family may appear somewhat comical and dysfunctional, but we are nothing less than beautifully balanced and delightfully different. With that said, my family stands guilty of many things, but we are not guilty of condemning anyone for his/her imperfections. Instead, we make it a priority to reeducate and redirect, encourage and console. Most importantly, the bond my family has is 100 percent solid because not only does the blood of Jesus covers us, it binds us!

By Sharon T. Anderson

Unless you are holding a gavel in one hand and the Book of Life in the other, **judge not**, for we all have flaws.

By Sharon T. Anderson

Morning Glory

Even during the natural light of day, others will forever throw shade; however, never let the gloom of others overshadow your glory.

By Sharon T. Anderson

Even the blind can see you are cut from
a different cloth; therefore stay
locked,
loaded, and
Under God's Armor.

By Sharon T. Anderson

Anything worth waiting for takes time; therefore,
until God gives the green light, I am **Gloriously Grounded**

By Sharon T. Anderson

I am hopeful.

I am humble.

I am still.

By Sharon T Anderson

Elders are the adhesive that keeps most families from falling apart. Therefore, never think you're running game or getting over, because once they become undone, you are pretty much doomed…**think!**

By Sharon T. Anderson

One who assumes, underestimates and/or deceptively tries to out-smart others will forever fail. With that said, rather than foolishly becoming a failure, be open, be honest and be frank. **Obtain the facts!**

By Sharon T. Anderson

Waiting on anyone other than my Lord and
Savior to instill peace will only result in
disappointment, for external sources cannot
create nor provide **internal peace**
so understand, what peace you seek only comes from within.

By Sharon T. Anderson

A
righ**T**eous

Person
n**E**ver worries
About what goes
publi**C**, because in private, he/she
do**E**s no wrong.

By Sharon T. Anderson

A Single Touch

O merciful Lord, today, I call on thee for more than just a word of counsel. I humbly seek healing. Therefore, I beg you to rid my mind, my body and my soul of all mental, physical and spiritual ailments, abnormalities and impurities. Please transform those inconceivable periods of pain into showers of everlasting peace, comfort and contentment. Father, I ask you to mend what is broken and repair what is damaged. For every immoral thought, odious word and ungodly gesture, I plead forgiveness. For future transgressions and ill will, both known and unknown, I seek clemency. I implore of such divine blessings because not only do I wish to walk in your ways, I crave to stand before the King with a pure, loving heart. And under no circumstances can I achieve any of this without the power of your healing touch. With that said, O merciful Lord, before thee I humbly kneel, with a request of just a single touch. Amen.

By Sharon T. Anderson

Keep hope alive,
for those who remain hopeful have a greater chance of healing.

By Sharon T. Anderson

Fearful Facts

The amount of controlling power fear has is nothing less than great. Because of such, subjects deliberately bypass life-changing opportunities, miss or simply disregard them altogether. However, phobias maybe difficult to overcome, but not impossible. With that said, the timid must be ready, willing and able to either shake such feelings or build up enough courage to face their concerns head-on; otherwise, the chances of becoming lifelong prisoners are quite promising.

By Sharon T. Anderson

Never let **fear**
overshadow your
faith, for it will
only result in
failure.

By Sharon T. Anderson

A mask of confIdence
meaNs
noThing
whEn harboring a
heart of Guilt. With that said,
exeRcise
rIghteousness in
private, and never have To
worrY about what goes public.

By Sharon T. Anderson

If you are not in search of morals, values and beliefs,
Keep Looking,
cause you are certainly not seeking me!

By Sharon T. Anderson

There will be no ifs, ands or buts about it! So exclude the excuses and stop looking for outlets, because dwelling on the past will get you little to nowhere. It is unfortunate but disappointment is a part of life, life is full of choices and certain choices have unpleasant consequences as well as repercussions. However, how long are you going to sit and sulk before you decide to get up, get out and **Make It Happen?**

By Sharon T. Anderson

Never be a **Quitter!**
Stand Up!
Stand Out!
Be a Go-Getter!

By Sharon T. Anderson

Dirty Rotten Scoundrels

We all know a person or have had friends that cleverly worked their way into the lives of others strictly for financial security but when suspicious questions arose, accusations often went unanswered, were somehow blown off or they were simply denied altogether. Meanwhile, those days of instant attitudes and far-fetched excuses quickly rolled into weeks, weeks turned into months and months regrettably transformed into long drawn-out years and still, there was no progress. However, thanks to Father Time and his mysterious way of revealing such devious intent, most of these dirty rotten scoundrels were cutoff without question or a hint of concern. With that said, exercise caution at all times because nowadays, freeloaders are not just looking for temporary assistance or a one time helping hand. They are seriously seeking lifelong support, freebies and never ending handouts.

By Sharon T. Anderson

I would rather be torn by truth

           than

                 taken by lies so please,

Spare Me Not!

By Sharon T. Anderson

I Am Me

I am what no other could ever be...I am me.
    So if it's just me being me that's causing you such insufferable grief,
        maybe you should flee, 'cause I am and will
    forever be...none other than just me!

By Sharon T. Anderson

No Nonsense

I refuse to feed into nonsense; therefore, if you
don't have all the facts, do me a favor and
miss me with the foolishness!

By Sharon T. Anderson

Express Yourself

Many simply miss their window of opportunity by beating around the bush, dropping hints or leaving clues. Let's be realistic! In this day and age, who has time for games of riddles and juvenile rhymes? Personally, it's a definite turnoff, because I am not looking for pre-school playmates, nor am I cruising for quick connections! I know what I want, and I refuse to settle for anything less. Therefore, man-up and **express yourself** like a mature, intelligent adult; otherwise, step aside and forever hold your peace.

By Sharon T. Anderson

Either **step up,**
or
step aside and let someone else **step in!**

By Sharon T. Anderson

Officially Free

Although we once laid cheek-to-cheek,
    what we had will never again be!

I'm not sure of what you really seek,
    but I'm absolutely certain it's definitely not me.

You love commotion.
    I crave peace.

You lack vision.
    I have needs.

Maybe it's you. Perhaps it's me.
    The fact remains, we never agree.

So forget the reason and save the speech.
    Retrieve your belongings and return the key.

No need to stand in disbelief,
    cause from this day forward, you're officially free!

By Sharon T. Anderson

The Repeat

After it's over and done, under no circumstances should one double back unless he/she has the stomach to ingest a double dose.

By Sharon T. Anderson

A man of excuses **will** remain useless,

but one who tries has the **power** to rise.

By Sharon T. Anderson

Have the **Heart** to let it **Beat!**

Live
Love
Laugh

By Sharon T. Anderson

A Divine Solution

Heavenly Father, not once was it written that life would be easy, fair or just; however, who would have thought life would be so hard? Because of such, I come to thee as humbly as I know how, O Lord. I come to thee in need of peace, stability and assurance. I come to thee, because no other has the power or the ability to fulfill such promises. Lord, I come to thee, because sometimes it feels as if I am fighting a losing battle, especially when I reflect on the amount of times I have been setback, turned away or simply denied. I come to thee, because just as the equation starts appear perfectly aligned and beautifully balanced, an unforeseen factor arises, tilts the table and cause a downward shift, and it is posing a definite problem. Messiah, I come to thee, because I am certain you have a divine solution for every discouraging dilemma, for every sad situation and for every mountain that needs moving! I come to thee, O Lord, because your unconditional love and devotion is what keeps me faithfully afloat and I do thank you. Amen

By Sharon T. Anderson

Trust

and

Believe

By Sharon T. Anderson

Be more than just another piece of arm and/or eye candy.
Be the **Beauty** and the **Brains.**

By Sharon T. Anderson

Knockout the kinks before they occur.
Think Ahead!

By Sharon T. Anderson

No Free Rides

Being an adult is more than just having a fully formed physique and/or being of legal age. It is a mature state of mind, a mindset of reasoning, responsibility and problem solving. It's about making sound decisions, honoring your word and prioritizing, especially under extreme pressure. Being an adult involves more than just playing the part. One must own the role. It's getting rid of those age-old security blankets and permanently doing away with safety nets. Now that you have an idea of what adulthood really entails, refrain from throwing temper tantrums and having hissy fits when things fail to go your way. Cease with the unnecessary outbursts (I'm grown) every time there is a misunderstanding and/or disagreement. Most importantly, stop acting like an immature adolescent and start behaving like an adult because in this life, there are no free rides!

By Sharon T. Anderson

When dealing with those who claim to know it all,
it's best to occasionally **step back** and let nature take its course.
Otherwise, how will they ever learn?

By Sharon T. Anderson

Start each day with energy of optimism, vivacious vibes and words of kindness, for darkness has no place in **a world of light**.

By Sharon T. Anderson

Stand in light
or
forever **Fall** in darkness!

By Sharon T. Anderson

Pose No Threat

If we pose no threat, why are we forever being scrutinized, taken to the limit and then pushed beyond boundaries without sufficient evidence or probable cause? Enlighten me...Mr. Man! Why are you so determined to bound, gag and illegally detain anyone that doesn't look like you, sound like you or act like you and your self-righteous crew, if we pose no threat? These are things I really need to know because in your eyes, not only are we irrelevant and have no potential, we are incapable of succeeding and just overall worthless and if that deems true, why won't you face us like the soldier you claim to be instead of sliding in like a petty thief during the night? Enlighten me, Mr. Man! Why are your unscrupulous behavior so acceptable and we are indisputably frowned upon? Why do you flinch the second we roar and then flee the moment we rise, and yet, we pose no threat? So before you try dishing out unwarranted commands, remember, we are the rightful Kings and Queens of this land, Mr. Man!

By Sharon T. Anderson

If I'm so worthless,
why fear my rising?

By Sharon T. Anderson

Planning with Purpose

It does not matter if it's work-related or regarding a relationship, because the same concept applies. Therefore, never panic or become discouraged when progress comes to a standstill. Instead, take a deep breath, buckle down and strategize. Create a plan that will increase your chances of making a greater comeback, one that is pertinent, powerful and foolproof. Make it a priority to standout, especially when the perfect opportunity presents itself. Leave a few memorable moments behind as an extra bonus to help seal the deal. Follow up with a confident call of persuasion: politely push, never pressure. Afterwards, give it to God and let go, because the plans He has for you may be quite different from what you have for yourself!

By Sharon T. Anderson.

God's plan has purpose.
Trust it!

By Sharon T. Anderson

Basic Instincts

In the midst of optimism, there is always one who secretly harbors hatred, a person who hides behind a warm smile and compelling voice, an individual who appears angelic but has negative or adverse vibes, vibes that tend to go ignored and often result in grief, a grief that is indisputably preventable if only you believe. With that said, if you are a person of belief and in need of clarity, tap into your God given instincts, listen carefully and then exercise complete trust. In doing so, not only will you perceive things differently, but the way in which you react to negativity will change as well. Furthermore, keep in mind that not all circles are rock solid just because they appear tight!

By Sharon T. Anderson

Beware of the company you keep,
for not all servants are saints.

By Sharon T. Anderson

Skeletons

You can try concealing them, uprooting or destroying them. You can even take a stab at burying them beneath tons of toxic rubble. However, hellacious secretes and fabricated lies are much like over fertilized weeds. They have a peculiar way of breaking through rock-solid surfaces in order to find light. Therefore, exercise honesty and plant the truth!

By Sharon T. Anderson

God will

exp**O**se all

Darkness

By Sharon T. Anderson

A Jumping Jubilee

It's gonna be more than just a toe tapping, hand clapping fun filled day. It's gonna be a jumping jubilee, you best believe partay!

So save the chitter-chatter, lessen the jibber jabber and let's get loose, for today is the day I break out the albums, turn up the volume and raise the roof!

Now go dim the lights, greet the invites and then pop the champagne. Get out and mingle, grab a handful of singles, and let it rain, let it rain!

Again, it's gonna be more than just a splashin' by the pool, kickin' it old school kind of day. It's gonna be a rump shakin', record breakin', underground reggae partay!

What did I say? It's gonna be more than just another wet-n-wild, spittin' it freestyle, shootin' the shit kind of day. It's gonna be a jumping jubilee, you best believe partay!

So miss me with the flimflam, forget about the shim sham and let's get this party started, cause today is the day I break out the albums, turn up the volume and rock to Bob Marley!

By Sharon T. Anderson

If you think I am

vivacioUs
thrilliNg
Spontaneous
High-spiriTed
animAted
BuBbly
Lively and
EnergEtic

now, you have yet to see the best!

By Sharon T. Anderson

Hearts of Harmony

How often do you find yourself bending over backwards, moving mountains or overextending your kindness for someone who rarely returns a simple phone call? How many times have you been left alone or was suddenly abandoned during moments of darkness, desperation or despair, by the very person who swore to never leave your side and yet, you just cannot seem to breakaway or put a definite end to that one-sided relationship? If the above scenario sounds familiar in any possible way, you are unfortunately stuck in a viscous cycle of self-inflicted torture, which stops now! Therefore, I call on you, O Lord. I ask that you bless these subjects with the willpower to walk away, the strength to stand firm and the confidence to never double back. I pray that you grant each one comfort, compatibility, unequivocal love and never-ending loyalty. Heavenly father, I beg you of these glorious gifts, because every beautiful heart deserves a lifetime of everlasting harmony, and through you, not only are these things possible, but they shall come to pass! Amen. (King James Version, Philippians 4:13)

By Sharon T. Anderson

Believing Is Achieving

There's not an obstacle I can't overcome or a barrier I can't break, for Christ is my source of power and in Him, I have faith. So don't tell me what's impossible! Stop telling me it can't be done, for I am the victor of battles, the conqueror of what's to come! (King James Version, Philippians 4:13)

By Sharon T. Anderson

Not Once

It is an utter disgrace to give false hope, especially if others rely on you for support. I say this because many portray to be things they are not until it's time to pay the piper and then most flee, fold or quickly accept defeat. However, although such acts have been taking place since the beginning of time, not once did my heavenly Father lose faith, surrender, compromise or ever break during the course of His life as a mortal. Not once did my Lord and Savior take flight, seek cover, deviate or disobey the divine word of God! Not once did Yahshua display signs of animosity or speak of regret, although He knew the outcome would be far less than favorable! However, what moves me the most was His extraordinary ability to exercise self-control throughout those inconceivable periods of pain and suffering. Even after Christ was crucified, He remains merciful, loving, understanding and kind. Most importantly, according to the scriptures, not once did the Son of David fail in any conceivable way, and under no circumstance should you! Therefore, stop wallowing in self-pity, making excuses and blaming others for your downfall! Stop giving them the power to steer you in the direction they find beneficial, and let the Redeemer take the wheel! That said, stand up, stand out and make a profound difference! Furthermore, wake up and become the man/woman that Almighty God created you to be!

By Sharon T. Anderson

Lighten the Load

Being yourself is much easier than living a life of lies,
so step into the light and exhale.

By Sharon T. Anderson

God's Favor

As long as you live, there will be obstacles to overcome, barriers to breakdown and challenges to face. There will be days of disappointment as well as moments of madness. The enemy will even try slithering in with words of deceit, discouragement and negativity, especially when you are on the verge of receiving life-changing blessings. However, never heed to those who plant poisonous seeds because where there is a will, God will make a definite and divine way. Therefore, remain faithful, focused and highspirited. Most importantly, put God first and you will forever have his undying favor!

By Sharon T. Anderson

No matter how high of a barrier the enemy may build or how deep of a ditch one digs, let nothing impede your path to greener pastures. **Stay Focused.**

By Sharon T. Anderson

Be the **base of support** your child deserves
and the foundation on which
he/she stands, for a child without stability has little to no chance!

By Sharon T. Anderson

As a nurturer, I will give my all. I will go above
and beyond to ensure pure happiness. I
will also make it a priority to be there through
both good and bad times. Above all else, I
will love unconditionally. However, I refuse to
argue with minors, especially my own;
therefore, when I say, "move" that's what I mean!
Furthermore, you better recognize,
cause I'm **Strictly Old Skool!**

By Sharon T. Anderson

A mouth that constantly moves never hears the **Voice of Reason.**
Therefore, take a moment to think before you act or speak!

By Sharon T. Anderson

Sometimes, there is
more power in
exercising silence than it is to roar.

Listen!

By Sharon T. Anderson

Just because it's free and appears fabulous, doesn't mean it's of goodness and glory. Therefore, **be mindful** of what you accept, for not all gifts come from God!

By Sharon T. Anderson

Heavenly Father, I cannot thank you enough
for the glorious gift of life, the
freedom of choice and the sense to **choose wisely.**

By Sharon T. Anderson

There is no greater challenge than challenging yourself...
raise the bar!

By Sharon T. Anderson

I fumble.
I fall.
I cry.
I cleanse.
I'm up.
I'm out.
I **try** again.

By Sharon T. Anderson

As a loyal Disciple of Christ, I will not
deviate from the plan, nor will I
allow anyone other than my Lord and Savior dictate my schedule!
Therefore, if you are coming as a distraction,
you will quickly be dismissed.
Furthermore, come correct or do not come at all,
because my house, **God Comes First!**

By Sharon T. Anderson

Kneel

No one stands taller,
sits higher
or roars louder than the **Supreme Being;**
therefore, humbly kneel before the **King!**

By Sharon T. Anderson

I Thirst

I am nowhere near perfect, nor do I claim or pretend to be. However, I crave compatibility like I hunger for a halo, which means, I have an extraordinary appetite and a thirst that only Christ can quench. Because of such, I refuse to settle for a sidepiece when I am clearly entitled to a full course meal. You see...I am not looking for a person of popularity, nor will I keep the company of a body that is forever at rest. Therefore, until those magical moments arise when two souls come together and happily harmonize, I will do nothing more than faithfully stay afloat!

By Sharon T. Anderson

I am indisputably in

Loyal

cOmmitted

deVoted

dEdicated

with my Lord and Savior, Jesus Christ!

By Sharon T. Anderson

Settle the Score

You know as well as I that what's good for the goose is also good for the gander. However, I refuse to go back and forth, nor will I play tit for tat. Then again, if you're serious about settling the score, I welcome the idea of going ten rounds in the ring, head to head. So bring it or back down, cause it's going to be a fight to the finish!

PS, either roll with the punches or risk being ran over!

By Sharon T. Anderson

If you show up and decide to show out,
be prepared
for the ultimate showdown!

By Sharon T. Anderson

His Chosen Path

Although I am blind to what my Savior foresees,
     I will forever follow the path that He has chosen for me.

By Sharon T. Anderson

**Indulge
in the
Light of the Lord**

By Sharon T. Anderson

Not for Sale

Many are under the impression that money has the purchasing power to work wonders regardless of time, item or need. And that may very well be true for anyone in the moneymaking business. However, God neither a buyer nor seller, which means; He will never break, bargain or take bribes. Therefore, it does not matter if you are a man of millions, a high roller or someone that is fashionably fabulous, because if you are not of goodness and glory, you have a better chance at breaking down the door of the devil than you do walking through the gates of heaven. With that said, why risk losing a possible place in paradise for a quick or temporary fix?

By Sharon T. Anderson

As long as I have life,
I will forever **live for the Lord.**

By Sharon T. Anderson

A Miraculous Makeover

A person of compassion has the ability to sympathize with those even when it is obvious he/she will never receive an ounce of sympathy in return. Consciously, a person of compassion could never bypass the needy without spreading words of kindness, instilling hope or lending a helping hand. Father, I can honestly to say, "I was once that pious person." However, after constantly being taken by lies and deceit, I have unfortunately become somewhat apprehensive. Because of such, a miraculous makeover is what I humbly beg of thee, O Lord. Soften my heart, alter my perception or reconfigure my entire outlook. Do whatever you deem necessary, for I only wish to walk in your ways.

By Sharon T. Anderson

I keep to myself **not** because I am antisocial,
but because when I lend a
helping hand, I can never get **one** in return.

By Sharon T. Anderson

In All Honesty

Sometimes it takes the bold and the honest to speak truth, someone who has no connections, nothing to lose and are not afraid of retaliation. It takes a person of gumption to abruptly remove the blinders of nonbelievers, reveal the obvious and clear the path to greener pastures, an individual who would rather speak truth than spare feelings, one who you would least expect when it comes to giving a clear, concise reality check. With that said, are you a self-imposed prisoner of denial, or one who welcomes the opportunity to face the facts?

By Sharon T. Anderson

News Flash

According to the forecast, I will forever be an outstanding

O...outspoken
U...unchanging
T...tenacious
C...clear-cut
A...authentic
S...spirited
T...tough

By Sharon T. Anderson

Fabricated Foolishness

Every family has a relative who over-exaggerates, one who are indisputably popular for capturing the attention of the crowd with either fabricated foolishness or flat-out lies. And when confronted, even then, he/she has a reason for every season, a slew of excuses and is inclined to lie without a moments delay. Still, we attentively listen, egg them on and often engage instead of easing away or abruptly shutting them down, which in my opinion, makes us just as guilty. With that said, where do you draw the line or put such madness to an end?

By Sharon T. Anderson

No matter how many versions a lie may produce or how fast they travel, **truth** will forever outshine darkness.

By Sharon T. Anderson

There's nothing like being **A Delight** in God's eyesight.

By Sharon T. Anderson

Levels of Learning

1. Most hear, but fail to listen.
2. Many listen, but do not comprehend.
3. Some comprehend, but refuse to heed.
4. A few heed to avoid the repeat.

Which best describes you and what can you do to self-improve?

By Sharon T. Anderson

CPSIA information can be obtained
at www.ICGtesting.com
Printed in the USA
LVHW041222110820
662878LV00003B/269